Human Behavior
And
Social Environment

By

Roshdy Ebrahim, Ph.D

2020

Human behavior and social environment

Copyright © 2020 Roshdy Ebrahim

ISBN: 9798603205021

Contents

Chapter 1
Is the world getting better or worse? [1]

Many people face the news each morning with trepidation and dread. Every day, we read of shootings, inequality, pollution, dictatorship, war and the spread of nuclear weapons. These are some of the reasons that 2016 was called the "Worst. Year. Ever." Until 2017 claimed that record and left many people longing for earlier decades, when the world seemed safer, cleaner and more equal.

But is this a sensible way to understand the human condition in the 21st century? As Franklin Pierce Adams pointed out, "Nothing is more responsible for the good old days than a bad memory."

You can always fool yourself into seeing a decline if you compare bleeding headlines of the present with rose-tinted images of the past. What does the trajectory of the

---

[1] steven pinker: Enlightenment Now: The Case for Reason, Science, Humanism, and Progress. Amazon, 2018

world look like when we measure well-being over time using a constant yardstick?

Let's compare the most recent data on the present with the same measures 30 years ago. Last year, Americans killed each other at a rate of 5.3 per hundred thousand, had seven percent of their citizens in poverty and emitted 21 million tons of particulate matter and four million tons of sulfur dioxide. But 30 years ago, the homicide rate was 8.5 per hundred thousand, poverty rate was 12 percent and we emitted 35 million tons of particulate matter and 20 million tons of sulfur dioxide.

What about the world as a whole? Last year, the world had 12 ongoing wars, 60 autocracies, 10 percent of the world population in extreme poverty and more than 10,000 nuclear weapons. But 30 years ago, there were 23 wars, 85 autocracies, 37 percent of the world population in extreme poverty and more than 60,000 nuclear weapons. True, last year was a terrible year for terrorism in Western

Europe, with 238 deaths, but 1988 was worse with 440 deaths.

What's going on? Was 1988 a particularly bad year? Or are these improvements a sign that the world, for all its struggles, gets better over time? Might we even invoke the admittedly old-fashioned notion of progress? To do so is to court a certain amount of derision, because I have found that intellectuals hate progress. And intellectuals who call themselves progressive really hate progress.

Now, it's not that they hate the fruits of progress, mind you. Most academics and pundits would rather have their surgery with anesthesia than without it. It's the idea of progress that rankles the chattering class. If you believe that humans can improve their lot, I have been told, that means that you have a blind faith and a quasi-religious belief in the outmoded superstition and the false promise of the myth of the onward march of inexorable progress. You are a cheerleader for vulgar American can-doism, with the rah-rah spirit of boardroom ideology, Silicon Valley and the Chamber of Commerce. You are a practitioner of Whig history, a naive optimist, a Pollyanna and, of course, a Pangloss, alluding to the Voltaire character who declared, "All is for the best in the best of all possible worlds."

Well, Professor Pangloss, as it happens, was a pessimist. A true optimist believes there can be much better worlds than the one we have today. But all of this is irrelevant, because the question of whether progress has taken place is not a matter of faith or having an optimistic temperament or seeing the glass as half full. It's a testable hypothesis. For all their differences, people largely agree on what goes into human well-being: life, health, sustenance, prosperity, peace, freedom, safety, knowledge, leisure, happiness. All of these things can be measured. If they have improved over time, that, I submit, is progress.

Let's go to the data, beginning with the most precious thing of all, life. For most of human history, life expectancy at birth was around 30. Today, worldwide, it is more than 70, and in the developed parts of the world, more than 80. 250 years ago, in the richest countries of the world, a third of the children did not live to see their fifth birthday, before the risk was brought down a hundredfold. Today, that fate befalls less than six percent of children in the poorest countries of the world. Famine is one of the Four Horsemen of the Apocalypse. It could bring devastation to any part of the world. Today, famine has been banished to the most remote and war-ravaged regions. 200 years ago, 90 percent of the world's population subsisted in extreme poverty. Today, fewer than 10 percent of people do. For most of human history, the powerful states and empires were pretty much always at war with each other, and peace was a mere interlude between wars. Today, they are never at war with each other. The last great power war pitted the United States against China 65 years ago. More recently, wars of all kinds have become fewer and less deadly. The annual rate of war has fallen from about 22 per hundred thousand per year in the early '50s to 1.2 today. Democracy has suffered obvious setbacks in Venezuela, in Russia, in Turkey and is threatened by the rise of authoritarian populism in Eastern Europe and the United States. Yet the world has never been more democratic than it has been in the past decade, with two-thirds of the world's people living in democracies. Homicide rates plunge whenever anarchy and the code of vendetta are replaced by the rule of law. It happened when feudal Europe was brought under the control of centralized kingdoms, so that today a Western European has 1/35th the chance of being murdered compared to his medieval ancestors. It happened again in colonial New

England, in the American Wild West when the sheriffs moved to town, and in Mexico.

Indeed, we've become safer in just about every way. Over the last century, we've become 96 percent less likely to be killed in a car crash, 88 percent less likely to be mowed down on the sidewalk, 99 percent less likely to die in a plane crash, 95 percent less likely to be killed on the job, 89 percent less likely to be killed by an act of God, such as a drought, flood, wildfire, storm, volcano, landslide, earthquake or meteor strike, presumably not because God has become less angry with us but because of improvements in the resilience of our infrastructure. And what about the quintessential act of God, the projectile hurled by Zeus himself? Yes, we are 97 percent less likely to be killed by a bolt of lightning.

Before the 17th century, no more than 15 percent of Europeans could read or write. Europe and the United States achieved universal literacy by the middle of the 20th century, and the rest of the world is catching up. Today, more than 90 percent of the world's population under the age of 25 can read and write. In the 19th century, Westerners worked more than 60 hours per week. Today, they work fewer than 40. Thanks to the universal penetration of running water and electricity in the developed world and the widespread adoption of washing machines, vacuum cleaners, refrigerators, dishwashers, stoves and microwaves, the amount of our lives that we forfeit to housework has fallen from 60 hours a week to fewer than 15 hours a week.

Do all of these gains in health, wealth, safety, knowledge and leisure make us any happier? The answer is yes. In 86 percent of the world's countries, happiness has increased in recent decades.

Well, I hope to have convinced you that progress is not a matter of faith or optimism, but is a fact of human history, indeed the greatest fact in human history. And how has this fact been covered in the news?

A tabulation of positive and negative emotion words in news stories has shown that during the decades in which humanity has gotten healthier, wealthier, wiser, safer and happier, the "New York Times" has become increasingly morose and the world's broadcasts too have gotten steadily glummer.

Why don't people appreciate progress? Part of the answer comes from our cognitive psychology. We estimate risk using a mental shortcut called the "availability heuristic." The easier it is to recall something from memory, the more probable we judge it to be. The other part of the answer comes from the nature of journalism, captured in this satirical headline from "The Onion," "CNN Holds Morning Meeting to Decide What Viewers Should Panic About for Rest of Day."

News is about stuff that happens, not stuff that doesn't happen. You never see a journalist who says, "I'm reporting live from a country that has been at peace for 40 years," or a city that has not been attacked by terrorists. Also, bad things can happen quickly, but good things aren't built in a day. The papers could have run the headline, "137,000 people escaped from extreme poverty yesterday" every day for the last 25 years. That's one and a quarter billion people leaving poverty behind, but you never read about it. Also, the news capitalizes on our morbid interest in what can go wrong, captured in the programming policy, "If it bleeds, it leads." Well, if you combine our cognitive biases with the nature of news, you can see why the world has been coming to an end for a very long time indeed.

Let me address some questions about progress that no doubt has occurred to many of you. First, isn't it good to be pessimistic to safeguard against complacency, to rake the muck, to speak truth to power? Well, not exactly. It's good to be accurate. Of course, we should be aware of suffering and danger wherever they occur, but we should also be aware of how they can be reduced, because there are dangers to indiscriminate pessimism. One of them is fatalism. If all our efforts at improving the world have been in vain, why throw good money after bad? The poor will always be with you. And since the world will end soon -- if climate change doesn't kill us all, then runaway artificial intelligence will -- a natural response is to enjoy life while we can, eat, drink and be merry, for tomorrow we die.

The other danger of thoughtless pessimism is radicalism. If our institutions are all failing and beyond hope for reform, a natural response is to seek to smash the machine, drain the swamp, burn the empire to the ground, on the hope that whatever rises out of the ashes is bound to be better than what we have now.

Well, if there is such a thing as progress, what causes it? Progress is not some mystical force or dialectic lifting us ever higher. It's not a mysterious arc of history bending toward justice. It's the result of human efforts governed by an idea, an idea that we associate with the 18th century Enlightenment, namely that if we apply reason and science that enhance human well-being, we can gradually succeed. Is progress inevitable? Of course not. Progress does not mean that everything becomes better for everyone everywhere all the time. That would be a miracle, and progress is not a miracle but problem-solving. Problems are inevitable and solutions create new problems which have to be solved in their turn. The unsolved problems facing the world today are gargantuan, including the risks of climate change and nuclear war, but we must see them as problems to be solved, not apocalypses in waiting, and aggressively pursue solutions like

Deep Decarbonization for climate change and Global Zero for nuclear war.

Finally, does the Enlightenment go against human nature? This is an acute question for me, because I'm a prominent advocate of the existence of human nature, with all its shortcomings and perversities. In my book "The Blank Slate," I argued that the human prospect is more tragic than utopian and that we are not stardust, we are not golden and there's no way we are getting back to the garden.

But my worldview has lightened up in the 15 years since "The Blank Slate" was published. My acquaintance with the statistics of human progress, starting with violence but now encompassing every other aspect of our well-being, has fortified my belief that in understanding our tribulations and woes, human nature is the problem, but human nature, channeled by Enlightenment norms and institutions, is also the solution.

Admittedly, it's not easy to replicate my own data-driven epiphany with humanity at large. Some intellectuals have responded with fury to my book "Enlightenment Now," saying first how dare he claim that intellectuals hate progress, and second, how dare he claim that there has been progress.

With others, the idea of progress just leaves them cold. Saving the lives of billions, eradicating disease, feeding the hungry, teaching kids to read? Boring.

At the same time, the most common response I have received from readers is gratitude, gratitude for changing their view of the world from a numb and helpless fatalism to something more constructive, even heroic.

I believe that the ideals of the Enlightenment can be cast a stirring narrative, and I hope that people with greater artistic flare and rhetorical power than I can tell it better and spread it further. It goes something like this.

We are born into a pitiless universe, facing steep odds against life-enabling order and in constant jeopardy of falling apart. We were shaped by a process that is ruthlessly competitive. We are made from crooked timber, vulnerable to illusions, self-centeredness and at times astounding stupidity.

Yet human nature has also been blessed with resources that open a space for a kind of redemption. We are endowed with the power to combine ideas recursively, to have thoughts about our thoughts. We have an instinct for language, allowing us to share the fruits of our ingenuity and experience. We are deepened with the capacity for sympathy, for pity, imagination, compassion, commiseration. These endowments have found ways to magnify their own power. The scope of language has been augmented by the written, printed and electronic word. Our circle of sympathy has been expanded by history, journalism and the narrative arts. And our puny rational faculties have been multiplied by the norms and institutions of reason, intellectual curiosity, open debate, skepticism of authority and dogma and the burden of proof to verify ideas by confronting them against reality.

As the spiral of recursive improvement gathers momentum, we eke out victories against the forces that grind us down, not least the darker parts of our own nature. We penetrate the mysteries of the cosmos, including life and mind. We live longer, suffer less, learn more, get smarter and enjoy more small pleasures and rich experiences. Fewer of us are killed, assaulted, enslaved, exploited or oppressed by the others. From a few oases, the territories with peace and prosperity are growing and could someday encompass the globe. Much suffering remains and tremendous peril, but ideas on how to reduce them have been voiced, and an infinite number of others are yet to be conceived.

We will never have a perfect world, and it would be dangerous to seek one. But there's no limit to the betterments we can attain if we continue to apply knowledge to enhance human flourishing. This heroic story is not just another myth. Myths are fictions, but this one is true, true to the best of our knowledge, which is the only truth we can have. As we learn more, we can show which parts of the story continue to be true and which ones false, as any of them might be and any could become.

And this story belongs not to any tribe but to all of humanity, to any sentient creature with the power of reason and the urge to persist in its being, for it requires only the convictions that life is better than death, health is better than sickness, abundance is better than want, freedom is better than coercion, happiness is better than suffering and knowledge is better than ignorance and superstition.

Chapter 2
What are the most important moral problems of our time? [2]

For the vast majority of human history, pretty much everyone lived on the equivalent of one dollar per day, and not much changed. But then, something extraordinary happened: The Scientific and Industrial Revolutions. And the basically flat graph you just saw transforms into this. What this graph means is that, in terms of power to change the world, we live in an unprecedented time in human history, and I believe our ethical understanding hasn't yet caught up with this fact. The Scientific and Industrial Revolutions transformed both our understanding of the world and our ability to alter it. What we need is an ethical revolution so that we can work out how do we use this

___

[2] William MacAskill: Doing Good Better: How Effective Altruism Can Help You Help Others, Do Work that Matters, and Make Smarter Choices about Giving Back. Amazon, 2016

tremendous bounty of resources to improve the world.

For the last 10 years, my colleagues and I have developed a philosophy and research program that we call effective altruism. It tries to respond to these radical changes in our world, uses evidence and careful reasoning to try to answer this question: How can we do the most good? Now, there are many issues you've got to address if you want to tackle this problem: whether to do good through your charity or your career or your political engagement, what programs to focus on, who to work with. But what I want to talk about is what I think is the most fundamental problem. Of all the many problems that the world faces, which should we be focused on trying to solve first? Now, I'm going to give you a framework for thinking about this question, and the framework is very simple. A problem's higher priority, the bigger, the more easily solvable and the more neglected it is. Bigger is better, because we've got more to gain if we do solve the problem. More easily solvable is better because I can solve the problem with less time or money. And most subtly, more neglected is better, because of diminishing returns. The more resources that have already been invested into solving a problem, the harder it will be to make additional progress. Now, the key thing that I want to leave with you is this framework, so that you can think for yourself what are the highest global priorities. But I and others in the effective altruism community have converged on three moral issues that we believe are unusually important, score unusually well in this framework.

First is global health. This is super solvable. We have an amazing track record in global health. Rates of death from measles, malaria, diarrheal disease are down by over 70 percent. And in 1980, we eradicated smallpox. I estimate we thereby saved over 60 million lives. That's more lives saved than if we'd achieved world peace in that same time period. On our current best estimates, we can save a life by distributing long-lasting insecticide-treated bed nets for just a few thousand dollars. This is an amazing opportunity.

The second big priority is factory farming. This is super neglected. There are 50 billion land animals used every year for food, and the vast majority of them are factory farmed, living in conditions of horrific suffering. They're probably among the worst-off creatures on this planet, and in many cases, we could significantly improve their lives for just pennies per animal. Yet this is hugely neglected. There are 3,000 times more animals in factory farms than there are stray pets, but yet, factory farming gets one fiftieth of the philanthropic funding. That means additional resources in this area could have a truly transformative impact.

Now the third area is the one that I want to focus on the most, and that's the category of existential risks: events like a nuclear war or a global pandemic that could permanently derail civilization or even lead to the extinction of the human race. Let me explain why I think this is such a big priority in terms of this framework.

First, size. How bad would it be if there were a truly existential catastrophe? Well, it would involve the deaths of all seven billion people on this planet and that means you and everyone you know and love. That's just a tragedy of unimaginable size. But then, what's more, it would also mean the curtailment of humanity's future potential, and I believe that humanity's potential is vast. The human race has been around for about 200,000 years, and if she lives as long as a typical mammalian species, she would last for about two million years. If the human race were a single individual, she would be just 10 years old today. And what's more, the human race isn't a typical mammalian species. There's no reason why, if we're careful, we should die off after only two million years. The earth will remain habitable for 500 million years to come. And if someday, we took to the stars, the civilization could continue for billions more.

So, I think the future is going to be really big, but is it going to be good? Is the human race even really worth preserving? Well, we hear all the time about how things have been getting worse, but I think that when we take the long run, things have been getting radically better. Here, for example, is life expectancy over time. Here's the proportion of people not living in extreme poverty. Here's the number of countries over time that have decriminalized homosexuality. Here's the number of countries over time that have become democratic. Then, when we look to the future, there could be so much more to gain again. We'll be so much richer; we can solve so many problems that are intractable today.

So, if this is kind of a graph of how humanity has progressed in terms of total human flourishing over time, well, this is what we would expect future progress to look like. It's vast.

Here, for example, is where we would expect no one to live in extreme poverty. Here is where we would expect everyone to be better off than the richest person alive today. Perhaps here is where we would discover the fundamental natural laws that govern our world. Perhaps here is where we discover an entirely new form of art, a form of music we currently lack the ears to hear. And this is just the next few thousand years. Once we think past that, well, we can't even imagine the heights that human accomplishment might reach.

So, the future could be very big and it could be very good, but are there ways we could lose this value? And sadly, I think there are. The last two centuries brought tremendous technological progress, but they also brought the global risks of nuclear war and the possibility of extreme climate change. When we look to the coming centuries, we should expect to see the same pattern again. And we can see some radically powerful technologies on the horizon. Synthetic biology might give us the power to create viruses of unprecedented contagiousness and lethality. Geoengineering might give us the power to dramatically alter the earth's climate. Artificial intelligence might give us the power to create intelligent agents with abilities greater than our own. Now, I'm not saying that any of these risks are particularly likely, but when there's so much at stake, even small probabilities matter a great deal. Imagine if you're getting on a plane and you're kind of nervous, and the pilot reassures you by saying, "There's only a one-in-a-thousand chance of crashing. Don't worry." Would you feel reassured? For these reasons, I think that preserving the future of humanity is among the most important problems that we currently face.

But let's keep using this framework. Is this problem neglected? And I think the answer is yes, and that's because problems that affect future generations are often hugely neglected. Why? Because future people don't participate in markets today. They don't have a vote. It's not like there's a lobby representing the interests of those born in 2300 AD. They don't get to influence the decisions we make today. They're voiceless. And that means we still spend a paltry amount on these issues: nuclear

nonproliferation, geoengineering,

biorisk, artificial intelligence safety. All of these receive only a few tens of millions of dollars of philanthropic funding every year. That's tiny compared to the 390 billion dollars that's spent on US philanthropy in total.

The final aspect of our framework then: Is this solvable? I believe it is. You can contribute with your money, your career or your political engagement. With your money, you can support organizations that focus on these risks, like the Nuclear Threat Initiative, which campaigns to take nuclear weapons off hair-trigger alert, or the Blue Ribbon Panel, which develops policy to minimize the damage from natural and man-made pandemics, or the Center for Human-Compatible AI, which does technical research to ensure that AI systems are safe and reliable. With your political engagement, you can vote for candidates that care about these risks, and you can support greater international cooperation. And then with your career, there is so much that you can do. Of course, we need scientists and policymakers and organization leaders, but just as importantly, we also need accountants and managers and assistants to work in these organizations that are tackling these problems.

Now, the research program of effective altruism is still in its infancy, and there's still a huge amount that we don't know. But even with what we've learned so far, we can see that by thinking carefully and by focusing on those problems that are big, solvable and neglected, we can make a truly tremendous difference to the world for thousands of years to come.

Chapter 3
Why I have coffee with people who send me hate mail [3]

My inbox is full of hate mails and personal abuse and has been for years. In 2010, I started answering those mails and suggesting to the writer that we might meet for coffee and a chat. I have had hundreds of encounters. They have taught me something important that I want to share with you.

I was born in Turkey from Kurdish parents and we moved to Denmark when I was a young child. In 2007, I ran for a seat in the Danish parliament as one of the first women with a minority background. I was elected, but I soon found out that not everyone was happy about it as I had to quickly get used to finding hate messages in my inbox. Those emails would begin with something like this: "What's a raghead like you doing in our parliament?" I never answered. I'd just delete the emails. I just

---

[3] ozlem cekic: bridge builder, author.

thought that the senders and I had nothing in common. They didn't understand me, and I didn't understand them. Then one day, one of my colleagues in the parliament said that I should save the hate mails. "When something happens to you, it will give the police a lead." I noticed that she said, "When something happens" and not "if."

Sometimes hateful letters were also sent to my home address. The more I became involved in public debate, the more hate mail and threats I received. After a while, I got a secret address and I had to take extra precautions to protect my family. Then in 2010, a Nazi began to harass me. It was a man who had attacked Muslim women on the street. Over time, it became much worse. I was at the zoo with my children, and the phone was ringing constantly. It was the Nazi. I had the impression that he was close. We headed home. When we got back, my son asked, "Why does he hate you so much, Mom, when he doesn't even know you?" "Some people are just stupid," I said. And at the time, I actually thought that was a pretty clever answer. And I suspect that that is the answer most of us would give. The others -- they are stupid, brainwashed, ignorant. We are the good guys and they are the bad guys, period.

Several weeks later I was at a friend's house, and I was very upset and angry about all the hate and racism I had met. It was he who suggested that I should call them up and visit them. "They will kill me," I said. "They would never attack a member of the Danish Parliament," he said. "And anyway, if they killed you, you would become a martyr."

"So, it's pure win-win situation for you." His advice was so unexpected, when I got home, I turned on my computer and opened the folder where I had saved all the hate mail. There were literally hundreds of them. Emails that started with words like "terrorist," "raghead," "rat," "whore." I decided to contact the one who had sent me the most. His name was Ingolf. I decided to contact him just once so I could say at least I had tried. To my surprise and shock, he answered the phone. I blurted out, "Hello, my name is Özlem. You have sent me so many hate mails. You don't know me; I don't know you. I was wondering if I could come around and we can drink a coffee together and talk about it?"

There was silence on the line. And then he said, "I have to ask my wife." What? The racist has a wife?

A couple of days later, we met at his house. I will never forget when he opened his front door and reached out to shake my hand. I felt so disappointed.

because he looked nothing like I'd imagined. I had expected a horrible person -- dirty, messy house. It was not. His house smelled of coffee which was served from a coffee set identical to the one my parents used. I ended up staying for two and a half hours. And we had so many things in common. Even our prejudices were alike.

Ingolf told me that when he waits for the bus and the bus stops 10 meters away from him, it was because the driver was a "raghead." I recognized that feeling. When I was young and I waited for the bus and it stopped 10 meters away from me, I was sure that the driver was a racist.

When I got home, I was very ambivalent about my experience. On the one hand, I really liked Ingolf. He was easy and pleasant to talk to, but on the other hand, I couldn't stand the idea of having so much in common with someone who had such clearly racist views. Gradually, and painfully, I came to realize that I had been just as judgmental of those who had sent me hate mails as they had been of me.

This was the beginning of what I call #dialogue coffee. Basically, I sit down for coffee with people who have said the most terrible things to me to try to understand why they hate people like me when they don't even know me. I have been doing this the last eight year. The vast majority of people I approach agree to meet me. Most of them are men, but I have also met women. I have made it a rule to always meet them in their house to convey from the outset that I trust them. I always bring food because when we eat together, it is easier to find what we have in common and make peace together.

Along the way, I have learned some valuable lessons. The people who sent hate mails are workers, husbands, wives, parents like you and me. I'm not saying that their behavior is acceptable, but I have learned to distance myself from the hateful views without distancing myself from the person who's expressing those views. And I have discovered that the people I visit are just as afraid of people they don't know as I was afraid of them before I started inviting myself for coffee.

During these meetings, a specific theme keeps coming up. It shows up regardless whether I'm talking to a humanist or a racist, a man, a woman, a Muslim or an atheist. They all seem to think that other people are to blame for the hate and for the generalization of groups. They all believe that other people have to stop demonizing. They point at politicians, the media, their neighbor or the bus driver who stops 10 meters away. But when I asked, "What about you? What can you do?", the reply is usually, "What can I do? I have no influence. I have no power." I know that feeling. For a large part of my life, I also thought that I didn't have any power or influence -- even when I was a member of the Danish parliament. But today I know the reality is different. We all have power and influence where we are, so we must never, never underestimate our own potential.

The #dialogue coffee meetings have taught me that people of all political convictions can be caught demonizing the others with different views. I know what I'm talking about. As a young child, I hated different population groups. And at the time, my religious views were very extreme. But my friendship with Turks, with Danes, with Jews and with racists has vaccinated me against my own prejudices. I grew up in a working-class family, and on my journey, I have met many people who have insisted on speaking to me. They have changed my views. They have formed me as a democratic citizen and a bridge builder. If you want to prevent hate and violence, we have to talk to as many people as possible for as long as possible while being as open as possible. That can only be achieved through debate, critical conversation and insisting on dialogue that doesn't demonize people.

I'm going to ask you a question. I invite you to think about it when you get home and in the coming days, but you have to be honest with yourself. It should be easy, no one else will know it. The question is this ... who do you demonize? Do you think supporters of American President Trump are deplorables? Or that those who voted for Turkish President Erdoğan are crazy Islamists? Or that those who voted for Le Pen in France are stupid fascists? Or perhaps you think that Americans who voted for Bernie Sanders are immature hippies.

All those words have been used to vilify those groups. Maybe at this point, do you think I am an idealist?

I want to give you a challenge. Before the end of this year, I challenge you to invite someone who you demonize -- someone who you disagree with politically and/or culturally and don't think you have anything in common with. I challenge you to invite someone like this to #dialogue coffee. Remember Ingolf? Basically, I'm asking you to find an Ingolf in your life, contact him or her and suggest that you can meet for #dialogue cofee.

When you start at #dialogue coffee, you have to remember this: first, don't give up if the person refuses at first. Sometimes it's taken me nearly one year to arrange a #dialogue coffee meeting. Two: acknowledge the other person's courage. It isn't just you who's brave. The one who's inviting you into their home is just as brave. Three: don't judge during the conversation. Make sure that most of the conversation focuses on what you have in common. As I said, bring food. And finally, remember to finish the conversation in a positive way because you are going to meet again. A bridge can't be built in one day.

We are living in a world where many people hold definitive and often extreme opinions about the others without knowing much about them. We notice of course the prejudices on the other side than in our own bases. And we ban them from our lives. We delete the hate mails. We hang out only with people who think like us and talk about the others in a category of disdain. We unfriend people on Facebook, and when we meet people who are discriminating or dehumanizing people or groups, we don't insist on speaking with them to challenge their opinions. That's how healthy democratic societies break down -- when we don't check the personal responsibility for the democracy. We take the democracy for granted. It is not. Conversation is the most difficult thing in a democracy and also the most important.

So, here's my challenge. Find your Ingolf. Start a conversation. Trenches have been dug between people, yes, but we all have the ability to build the bridges that cross the trenches. And let me end by quoting my friend, Sergeot Uzan, who lost his son, Dan

Uzan, in a terror attack on a Jewish synagogue in Copenhagen, 2015. Sergio rejected any suggestion of revenge and instead said this ... "Evil can only be defeated by kindness between people. Kindness demands courage." Dear friends, let's be courageous.

Chapter 4
Why it's worth listening to people you disagree with [4]

In 1994, Charles Murray and Richard Herrnstein coauthored "The Bell Curve," an extremely controversial book which claims that on average, some races are smarter and more likely to succeed than others. Murray and Herrnstein also suggest that a lack of critical intelligence explains the prominence of violent crime in poor African-American communities. But Charles Murray and Richard Herrnstein are not the only people who think this.

In 2012, a writer, journalist and political commentator named John Derbyshire wrote an article that was supposed to be a non-black version of the talk that many black parents feel they have to give their kids today: advice on how to stay safe. In it, he

---

)[4] Zachary R.wood: Uncensored: My Life and Uncomfortable Conversations at the Intersection of Black and White America. Amazon 2018

offered suggestions such as: "Do not attend events likely to draw a lot of blacks," "Stay out of heavily black neighborhoods" and "Do not act the Good Samaritan to blacks in distress." And yet, in 2016, I invited John Derbyshire as well as Charles Murray to speak at my school, knowing full well that I would be giving them a platform and attention for ideas that I despised and rejected. But this is just a further evolution of a journey of uncomfortable learning throughout my life.

When I was 10 years old, my mother was diagnosed with schizophrenia, a mental illness characterized by mood swings and paranoid delusions. Throughout my life, my mother's rage would turn our small house into a minefield. Yet, though I feared her rage on a daily basis, I also learned so much from her. Our relationship was complicated and challenging, and at the age of 14, it was decided that I needed to live apart from her. But over the years, I've come to appreciate some of the important lessons my mother taught me about life. She was the first person who spoke to me about learning from the other side. And she, like me, was born and raised in a family of committed liberal democrats. Yet, she encouraged me to see the world and the issues our world faces as complex, controversial and ever-changing.

One day, I came across the phrase "affirmative action" in a book I was reading. And when I asked her what the term meant, she spent what felt like an hour giving me a thorough and thoughtful explanation that would make sense to a small child. She even made the topic sound at least as interesting as any of my professors have. She explained the many reasons why people of various political views challenge and support affirmative action, stressing that, while she strongly supported it herself, it was important for me to view the issue as a controversial one with a long history, a questionable future and a host of complicating factors. While affirmative action can increase the presence of minorities at elite educational institutions, she felt that it could also disadvantage hardworking people of different races from more affluent backgrounds. My mom wanted me to understand that I should never just write off opinions that I disagreed with or disliked, because there was always something to learn from the perspectives of others, even when doing so might be difficult.

But life at home with my mom was not the only aspect of my journey that has been formative and uncomfortable. In fourth grade, she decided that I should attend a private school in order to receive the best education possible. As a black student attending predominantly white private schools, I've encountered attitudes and behaviors that reflected racial stereotypes. Several of my friends' parents assumed within minutes of meeting me that my best skill was playing basketball. And it really upset me to think that my race made it harder for them to see me as a student who loved reading, writing and speaking. Experiences like this motivated me to work tirelessly to disprove what I knew people had assumed. My mother even said that, in order to put my best foot forward, I had to be patient, alert and excruciatingly well-mannered. To prove that I belonged, I had to show poise and confidence, the ability to speak well and listen closely. Only then would my peers see that I deserved to be there as much as they did.

Despite this racial stereotyping and the discomfort, I often felt, the learning I gained from other aspects of being at an elite private school were incredibly valuable. I was encouraged by my teachers to explore my curiosity, to challenge myself in new ways and to deepen my understanding of subjects that fascinated me the most. And going to college was the next step. I was excited to take my intellectual drive and interest in the world of ideas to the next level. I was eager to engage in lively debate with peers and professors and with outside speakers; to listen, to learn and gain a deeper understanding of myself and of others. While I was fortunate to meet peers and professors who were interested in doing the same thing, my desire to engage with difficult ideas was also met with resistance.

To prepare myself to engage with controversy in the real world, I joined a group that brought controversial speakers to campus. But many people fiercely opposed this group, and I received significant pushback from students, faculty and my administration. For many, it was difficult to see how bringing controversial speakers to campus could be valuable, when they caused harm. And it was disappointing to me facing personal attacks, having my administration cancel speakers and hearing my intentions distorted by those around me. My work also hurt the feelings of many, and I understood that. Of course, no one likes being offended, and I certainly don't like hearing controversial speakers argue that feminism has become a war against men or that blacks have lower IQs than whites. I also understand that some people have experienced traumatic experiences in their lives. And for some, listening to offensive views can be like reliving the very traumas that they've worked so hard to overcome. Many argue that by giving these people a platform, you're doing more harm than good, and I'm reminded of this every time I listen to these points of view and feel my stomach turn.

Yet, tuning out opposing viewpoints doesn't make them go away, because millions of people agree with them. In order to understand the potential of society to progress forward, we need to understand the counterforces. By engaging with controversial and offensive ideas, I believe that we can find common ground, if not with the speakers themselves, then with the audiences they may attract or indoctrinate. Through engaging, I believe that we may reach a better understanding, a deeper understanding, of our own beliefs and preserve the ability to solve problems, which we can't do if we don't talk to each other and make an effort to be good listeners.

But soon after I announced that John Derbyshire would be speaking on campus, student backlash erupted on social media. The tide of resistance, in fact, was so intense, that my college president rescinded the invitation. I was deeply disappointed by this because, as I saw it, there would be nothing that any of my peers or I could do to silence someone who agreed with him in the office environment of our future employers.

I look out at what's happening on college campuses, and I see the anger. And I get it. But what I wish I could tell people is that it's worth the discomfort, it's worth listening, and that we're stronger, not weaker, because of it. When I think about my experiences with uncomfortable learning, and I reflect upon them, I've found that it's been very difficult to change the values of the intellectual community that I've been a part of. But I do feel a sense of hope when I think about the individual interactions that I've been able to have with students who both support the work that I'm doing and who feel challenged by it and who do not support it. What I've found is that, while it can be difficult to change the values of a community, we can gain a lot from individual interactions.

While I didn't get to engage with John Derbyshire due to my president's disinvitation, I was able to have dinner with Charles Murray before his talk. I knew the conversation would be difficult. And I didn't expect it to be pleasant. But it was cordial, and I did gain a deeper understanding of his arguments. I found that he, like me, believed in creating a more just society. The thing is, his understanding of what justice entailed was very different from my own. The way in which he wanted to understand the issue, the way in which he wanted to approach the issue of inequality also differed from my own. And I found that his understanding of issues like welfare and affirmative action was tied and deeply rooted in his understanding of various libertarian and conservative beliefs, what diminishes and increases their presence in our society. While he expressed his viewpoints eloquently, I remained thoroughly unconvinced. But I did walk away with a deeper understanding.

It's my belief that to achieve progress in the face of adversity, we need a genuine commitment to gaining a deeper understanding of humanity. I'd like to see a world with more leaders who are familiar with the depths of the views of those they deeply disagree with, so that they can understand the nuances of everyone they're representing. I see this as an ongoing process involving constant learning, and I'm confident that I'll be able to add value down the line if I continue building empathy and understanding through engaging with unfamiliar perspectives.

Chapter 5
Our loss of wisdom [5]

In his inaugural address, Barack Obama appealed to each of us to give our best as we try to extricate ourselves from this current financial crisis. But what did he appeal to? He did not, happily, follow in the footsteps of his predecessor, and tell us to just go shopping. Nor did he tell us, "Trust us. Trust your country. Invest, invest, invest." Instead, what he told us was to put aside childish things. And he appealed to virtue. Virtue is an old-fashioned word. It seems a little out of place in a cutting-edge environment like this one. And besides, some of you might be wondering, what the hell does it mean?

Let me begin with an example. This is the job description of a hospital janitor that is scrolling up on the screen. And all of the items on it are unremarkable. They're the things you would expect: mop the floors, sweep them,

---

)[5] Barry schwartz: Why We Work (TED Books). Amazon, 2015

empty the trash, restock the cabinets. It may be a little surprising how many things there are, but it's not surprising what they are. But the one thing I want you to notice about them is this: even though this is a very long list, there isn't a single thing on it that involves other human beings. Not one. The janitor's job could just as well be done in a mortuary as in a hospital.

And yet, when some psychologists interviewed hospital janitors to get a sense of what they thought their jobs were like, they encountered Mike, who told them about how he stopped mopping the floor because Mr. Jones was out of his bed getting a little exercise, trying to build up his strength, walking slowly up and down the hall. And Charlene told them about how she ignored her supervisor's admonition and didn't vacuum the visitor's lounge because there were some family members who were there all day, every day who, at this moment, happened to be taking a nap. And then there was Luke, who washed the floor in a comatose young man's room twice because the man's father, who had been keeping a vigil for six months, didn't see Luke do it the first time, and his father was angry. And behavior like this from janitors, from technicians, from nurses and, if we're lucky now and then, from doctors, doesn't just make people feel a little better, it actually improves the quality of patient care and enables hospitals to run well.

Now, not all janitors are like this, of course. But the ones who are think that these sorts of human interactions involving kindness, care and empathy are an essential part of the job. And yet their job description contains not one word about other human beings. These janitors have the moral will to do right by other people. And beyond this, they have the moral skill to figure out what "doing right" means.

"Practical wisdom," Aristotle told us, "is the combination of moral will and moral skill." A wise person knows when and how to make the exception to every rule, as the janitors knew when to ignore the job duties in the service of other objectives. A wise person knows how to improvise, as Luke did when he re-washed the floor. Real-world problems are often ambiguous and ill-defined and the context is always changing. A wise person is like a jazz musician -- using the notes on the page, but dancing around them, inventing combinations that are appropriate for the situation and the people at hand. A wise person knows how to use these moral skills in the service of the right aims. To serve other people, not to manipulate other people. And finally, perhaps most important, a wise person is made, not born. Wisdom depends on experience, and not just any experience. You need the time to get to know the people that you're serving. You need permission to be allowed to improvise, try new things, occasionally to fail and to learn from your failures. And you need to be mentored by wise teachers.

When you ask the janitors, who behaved like the ones I described how hard it is to learn to do their job, they tell you that it takes lots of experience. And they don't mean it takes lots of experience to learn how to mop floors and empty trash cans. It takes lots of experience to learn how to care for people. The good news is you don't need to be brilliant to be wise. The bad news is that without wisdom, brilliance isn't enough. It's as likely to get you and other people into trouble as anything else.

Now, I hope that we all know this. There's a sense in which it's obvious, and yet, let me tell you a little story. It's a story about lemonade. A dad and his seven-year-old son were watching a Detroit Tigers game at the ballpark. His son asked him for some lemonade and Dad went to the concession stand to buy it. All they had was Mike's Hard Lemonade, which was five percent alcohol. Dad, being an academic, had no idea that Mike's Hard Lemonade contained alcohol. So, he brought it back. And the kid was drinking it, and a security guard spotted it, and called the police, who called an ambulance that rushed to the ballpark, whisked the kid to the hospital. The emergency room ascertained that the kid had no alcohol in his blood. And they were ready to let the kid go.

But not so fast. The Wayne County Child Welfare Protection Agency said no. And the child was sent to a foster home for three days. At that point, can the child go home? Well, a judge said yes, but only if the dad leaves the house and checks into a motel. After two weeks, I'm happy to report, the family was reunited. But the welfare workers and the ambulance people and the judge all said the same thing: "We hate to do it but we have to follow procedure."

How do things like this happen? Scott Simon, who told this story on NPR, said, "Rules and procedures may be dumb, but they spare you from thinking." And, to be fair, rules are often imposed because previous officials have been lax and they let a child go back to an abusive household. Fair enough. When things go wrong, as of course they do, we reach for two tools to try to fix them.

One tool we reach for is rules. Better ones, more of them. The second tool we reach for is incentives. Better ones, more of them. What else, after all, is there? We can certainly see this in response to the current financial crisis. Regulate, regulate, regulate. Fix the incentives, fix the incentives, fix the incentives ... The truth is that neither rules nor incentives are enough to do the job. How could you even write a rule that got the janitors to do what they did? And would you pay them a bonus for being empathic? It's preposterous on its face. And what happens is that as we turn increasingly to rules, rules and incentives may make things better in the short run, but they create a downward spiral that makes them worse in the long run. Moral skill is chipped away by an over-reliance on rules that deprives us of the opportunity to improvise and learn from our improvisations. And moral will be undermined by an incessant appeal to incentives that destroy our desire to do the right thing. And without intending it, by appealing to rules and incentives, we are engaging in a war on wisdom.

Let me just give you a few examples, first of rules and the war on moral skill. The lemonade story is one. Second, no doubt more familiar to you, is the nature of modern American education: scripted, lock-step curricula. Here's an example from Chicago kindergarten. Reading and enjoying literature and words that begin with 'B.' "The Bath:" Assemble students on a rug and give students a warning about the dangers of hot water. Say 75 items in this script to teach a 25-page picture book. All over Chicago in every kindergarten class in the city, every teacher is saying the same words in the same way on the same day. We know why these scripts are there. We don't trust the judgment of teachers enough to let them loose on their own. Scripts like these are insurance policies against disaster. And they prevent disaster. But what they assure in its place is mediocrity.

Don't get me wrong. We need rules! Jazz musicians need some notes -- most of them need some notes on the page. We need more rules for the bankers, God knows. But too many rules prevent accomplished jazz musicians from improvising. And as a result, they lose their gifts, or worse, they stop playing altogether.

Now, how about incentives? They seem cleverer. If you have one reason for doing something and I give you a second reason for doing the same thing, it seems only logical that two reasons are better than one and you're more likely to do it. Right? Well, not always. Sometimes two reasons to do the same thing seem to compete with one another instead of complimenting, and they make people less likely to do it.

I'll just give you one example because time is racing. In Switzerland, back about 15 years ago, they were trying to decide where to site nuclear waste dumps. There was going to be a national referendum. Some psychologists went around and polled citizens who were very well informed. And they said, "Would you be willing to have a nuclear waste dump in your community?" Astonishingly, 50 percent of the citizens said yes. They knew it was dangerous. They thought it would reduce their property values. But it had to go somewhere and they had responsibilities as citizens. The psychologists asked other people a slightly different question. They said, "If we paid you six weeks' salary every year would you be willing to have a nuclear waste dump in your community?" Two reasons. It's my responsibility and I'm getting paid. Instead of 50 percent saying yes, 25 percent said yes. What happens is that the second this introduction of incentive gets us so that instead of asking, "What is my responsibility?" all we ask is, "What serves my interests?" When incentives don't work, when CEOs ignore the long-term health of their companies in pursuit of short-term gains that will lead to massive bonuses, the response is always the same. Get smarter incentives.

The truth is that there are no incentives that you can devise that are ever going to be smart enough. Any incentive system can be subverted by bad will. We need incentives. People have to make a living. But excessive reliance on incentives demoralizes professional activity in two senses of that word. It causes people who engage in that activity to lose morale and it causes the activity itself to lose morality.

Barack Obama said, before he was inaugurated, "We must ask not just 'Is it profitable?' but 'Is it right?'" And when professions are demoralized, everyone in them becomes dependent on -- addicted to -- incentives and they stop asking "Is it right?" We see this in medicine. ("Although it's nothing serious, let's keep an eye on it to make sure it doesn't turn into a major lawsuit.") And we certainly see it in the world of business. ("In order to remain competitive in today's marketplace, I'm afraid we're going to have to replace you with a sleeze ball.") ("I sold my soul for about a tenth of what the damn things are going for now.") It is obvious that this is not the way people want to do their work.

So what can we do? A few sources of hope: we ought to try to re-moralize work. One way not to do it: teach more ethics courses. There is no better way to show people that you're not serious than to tie up everything you have to say about ethics into a little package with a bow and consign it to the margins as an ethics course.

What to do instead? One: Celebrate moral exemplars. Acknowledge, when you go to law school, that a little voice is whispering in your ear about Atticus Finch. No 10-year-old goes to law school to do mergers and acquisitions. People are inspired by moral heroes. But we learn that with sophistication comes the understanding that you can't acknowledge that you have moral heroes. Well, acknowledge them. Be proud that you have them. Celebrate them. And demand that the people who teach you acknowledge them and celebrate them too. That's one thing we can do.

I don't know how many of you remember this: another moral hero, 15 years ago, Aaron Feuerstein, who was the head of Malden Mills in Massachusetts -- they made Polartec -- The factory burned down. 3,000 employees. He kept every one of them on the payroll. Why? Because it would have been a disaster for them and for the community if he had let them go. "Maybe on paper our company is worth less to Wall Street, but I can tell you it's worth more. We're doing fine."

we heard talks from several moral heroes. Two were particularly inspiring to me. One was Ray Anderson, who turned, you know, a part of the evil empire into a zero-footprint, or almost zero-footprint business. Why? Because it was the right thing to do. And a bonus he's discovering is he's actually going to make even more money. His employees are inspired by the effort. Why? Because there happy to be doing something that's the right thing to do. Yesterday we heard Willie Smits talk about re-foresting in Indonesia.

In many ways this is the perfect example. Because it took the will to do the right thing. God knows it took a huge amount of technical skill. I'm boggled at how much he and his associates needed to know in order to plot this out. But most important to make it work -- and he emphasized this -- is that it took knowing the people in the communities. Unless the people you're working with are behind you, this will fail. And there isn't a formula to tell you how to get the people behind you, because different people in different communities organize their lives in different ways.

And you don't have to be a mega-hero. There are ordinary heroes. Ordinary heroes like the janitors who are worth celebrating too. As practitioners each and every one of us should strive to be ordinary, if not extraordinary heroes. As heads of organizations, we should strive to create environments that encourage and nurture both moral skill and moral will. Even the wisest and most well-meaning people will give up if they have to swim against the current in the organizations in which they work.

If you run an organization, you should be sure that none of the jobs -- none of the jobs -- have job descriptions like the job descriptions of the janitors. Because the truth is that any work that you do that involves interaction with other people is moral work. And any moral work depends upon practical wisdom.

And, perhaps most important, as teachers, we should strive to be the ordinary heroes, the moral exemplars, to the people we mentor. And there are a few things that we have to remember as teachers. One is that we are always teaching. Someone is always watching. The camera is always on. Bill Gates talked about the importance of education and, in particular, the model that KIPP was providing: "Knowledge is power." And he talked about a lot of the wonderful things that KIPP is doing to take inner-city kids and turn them in the direction of college.

I want to focus on one particular thing KIPP is doing that Bill didn't mention. That is that they have come to the realization that the single most important thing kids need to learn is character. They need to learn to respect themselves. They need to learn to respect their schoolmates. They need to learn to respect their teachers. And, most important, they need to learn to respect learning. That's the principle objective. If you do that, the rest is just pretty much a coast downhill. And the teachers: the way you teach these things to the kids is by having the teachers and all the other staff embody it every minute of every day.

Obama appealed to virtue. And I think he was right. And the virtue I think we need above all others is practical wisdom, because it's what allows other virtues -- honesty, kindness, courage and so on -- to be displayed at the right time and in the right way. He also appealed to hope. Right again. I think there is reason for hope. I think people want to be allowed to be virtuous.

Wanting to do the right thing in the right way for the right reasons. This kind of wisdom is within the grasp of each and every one of us if only we start paying attention. Paying attention to what we do, to how we do it, and, perhaps most importantly, to the structure of the organizations within which we work, so as to make sure that it enables us and other people to develop wisdom rather than having it suppressed.

Chapter 6
To solve the world's biggest problems, invest in women and girls [6]

My mother was a philanthropist She carried out her philanthropy in our community through a practice we call, "isirika." She supported the education of scores of children and invited many to live with us in our home in order to access schools. She mobilized resources for building the local health clinic and the maternity wing is named in memory of her. But most important, she was endeared by the community for her organizing skills, because she organized the community, and specifically women, to find solutions to anything that was needed.

She did all of this through isirika. Let me repeat that word for you again: isirika.

So, isirika is a pragmatic way of life that embraces charity, services and philanthropy all together. The essence of

---

)[6] Musimbi kanyoro: women's rights activist.

isirika is to make it clear to everybody that you're your sister's keeper -- and yes, you're your brother's keeper. Mutual responsibility for caring for one another. A literal, simple English translation would be equal generosity, but the deep philosophical meaning is caring, together, for one another.

So how does isirika really happen? I grew up in a farming community in western Kenya. I remember vividly the many times that neighbors would go to a neighbor's home -- a sick neighbor's home -- and harvest their crop for them. I tagged alongside with my mother to community events and to women's events, and had the conversation about vaccinations in school, building the health center and really big things -- renewing seeds for the next planting season. And often, the community would come together to contribute money to send a neighbor's child to school -- not only in the country but to universities abroad as well. And so we have a surgeon. The first surgeon in my country came from that rural village.

So ... what isirika did was to be inclusive. We as children would stand alongside the adults and give our contributions of money, and our names were in scripted in the community book just like every adult.

And then I grew up, went to universities back at home and abroad, obtained a few degrees here and there, became organized and took up international jobs, working in development, humanitarian work and philanthropy. And very soon, isirika began to become small. It dissipated and then just disappeared. In each place, I gained a new vocabulary. The vocabulary of donors and recipients. The vocabulary of measuring impact, return on investment ... projects and programs. Communities such as my childhood community became referred to as "poor, vulnerable populations." Those are the communities of which literature speaks about as living on less than a dollar a day, and they become the targets for poverty eradication programs. And by the way, they are the targets of our first United Nations' sustainable development goal. Now, I'm really interested that we find solutions to poverty and to the world's other many big problems because they do exist. I however think that we could do a better job, and we could do a better job by embracing isirika. So, let me tell you how.

First, isirika affirms common humanity. For whatever that you do, you begin from the premise that you're human together. When you begin that you're human together, you see each other differently. You don't see a refugee first and you don't see a woman first and you don't see a person with disability first. You see a human being first. That is the essence of seeing a person first. And when you do that, you value their ideas, you value their contribution -- small or big. And you value what they bring to the table. That is the essence of isirika.

I just want to imagine what it would look like if everyone in this room -- a medical doctor, a parent, a lawyer, a philanthropist, whatever you are -- if you embraced isirika and made it your default. What could we achieve for each other? What could we achieve for humanity? What could we achieve for peace issues? What could we achieve for medical science? Let me give you a couple of hints, because I'm going to ask you to accompany me in this process of rebuilding and reclaiming isirika with me.

First, you have to have faith that we are one humanity, we have one planet and we don't have two choices about that. So, there's not going to be a wall that is high enough to separate humanity. So, give up the walls. Give them up.

And we don't have a planet B to go to. So that's really important. Make that clear; move onto the next stage. The second stage: remember, in isirika, every idea count. Bridges have big posters and they have nails. Every idea count -- small or big counts. And third, isirika affirms that those who have more really enjoy the privilege of giving more. It is a privilege to give more.

And this is the time for women to give more for women. It is the time to give more for women. Our parents, when they brought in other children to live with us, they didn't ask our permission. They made it clear that they had a responsibility because they had gone to school and they had an earning. And they made it clear that we should understand that their prosperity was not our entitlement, and I think that's good wisdom from isirika. We could use that wisdom today, I think, in every culture, in every place, passing to the next generation what we could do together.

I have, over the years, encountered isirika in many places, but what gives me really the passion today to embrace isirika is the work that I do with women all over the world through the Global Fund for Women, though women's funds and through women's movements globally. If you work with women, you change every day because you experience them living isirika together in what they do.

In the work that I do, we trust women leaders and their ideas. And we support them with funding so that they can expand, they can grow and they can thrive within their own communities. A woman in 1990 came to the Global Fund with a big idea -- a woman from Mexico by the name of Lucero González. She wanted to begin a fund that would support a movement that would be rooted in the communities in Mexico. And she received a grant of 7,500 US dollars. Today, 25 years later, Semillas, the name of the fund, has raised and spent, within the community, 17.8 million dollars.

They have impacted over two million people, and they work with a group of 600,000 women in Mexico. During the recent earthquake, they were so well rooted that they could quickly assess within the community and with others, what were the short-term needs and what were the long-term needs. And I tell you, long after the lights have gone off Mexico, Semillas will be there with the communities, with the women, for a very long time. And that's what I'm talking about: when we are able to support the ideas of communities that are rooted within their own setting.

Thirty years ago, there was very little funding that went directly to women's hands in their communities. Today we celebrate 168 women's funds all over the world, 100 of which are in this country.

they support grassroots women's organizations -- community organizations under the leadership of girls and women, and together we have been able, collectively, to give a billion dollars to women and girls-led organizations.

But the challenge begins today. The challenge begins today because we see women everywhere organizing as isirika. Because isirika is the evergreen wisdom that lives in communities. You find it in indigenous communities, in rural communities. And what it really ingrains in people is that ability to trust and to move the agenda ahead.

So, three things that I have learned that I want to share with you through my work. One: if you want to solve the world's biggest problems, invest in women and girls.

Not only do they expand the investment, but they care for everyone in the community. Not only their needs but the needs of their children, the needs of the rest of the community, the needs of the elderly, and most important, they protect themselves -- which is really important -- and they protect their communities. Women who know how to protect themselves know what it means to make a difference. And the second reason that I'm asking you to invest in women and girls is because this is the smartest thing you could ever do at this particular time. And if we are going to have over 350 trillion dollars by 2030, those dollars need to be in the hands of women.

And so, I grew up with isirika. My mother was isirika. She was not a project or a program. And now, I pass that to you. That you will be able to share this with your families, with your friends and with your community, and embrace isirika as a way of living -- as a pragmatic way of living.

Chapter 7
Human trafficking is all around you [7]

About 10 years ago, I went through a little bit of a hard time. So, I decided to go see a therapist. I had been seeing her for a few months, when she looked at me one day and said, "Who actually raised you until you were three?" Seemed like a weird question. I said, "My parents." And she said, "I don't think that's actually the case; because if it were, we'd be dealing with things that are far more complicated than just this."

It sounded like the setup to a joke, but I knew she was serious. Because when I first started seeing her, I was trying to be the funniest person in the room. And I would try and crack these jokes, but she caught on to me really quickly, and whenever I tried to make a joke, she would look at me and say, "That is actually really sad." It's terrible.

)[7] Noy thrupkaew: global journalist.

So, I knew I had to be serious, and I asked my parents who had actually raised me until I was three? And to my surprise, they said my primary caregiver had been a distant relative of the family. I had called her my auntie.

I remember my auntie so clearly, it felt like she had been part of my life when I was much older. I remember the thick, straight hair, and how it would come around me like a curtain when she bent to pick me up; her soft, southern Thai accent; the way I would cling to her, even if she just wanted to go to the bathroom or get something to eat. I loved her, but [with] the ferocity that a child has sometimes before she understands that love also requires letting go.

But my clearest and sharpest memory of my auntie, is also one of my first memories of life at all. I remember her being beaten and slapped by another member of my family. I remember screaming hysterically and wanting it to stop, as I did every single time it happened, for things as minor as wanting to go out with her friends, or being a little late. I became so hysterical over her treatment, that eventually, she was just beaten behind closed doors.

Things got so bad for her that eventually she ran away. As an adult, I learned later that she had been just 19 when she was brought over from Thailand to the States to care for me, on a tourist visa. She wound up working in Illinois for a time, before eventually returning to Thailand, which is where I ran into her again, at a political rally in Bangkok. I clung to her again, as I had when I was a child, and I let go, and then I promised that I would call. I never did, though. Because I was afraid if I said everything that she meant to me -- that I owed perhaps the best parts of who I became to her care, and that the words "I'm sorry" were like a thimble to bail out all the guilt and shame and rage I felt over everything she had endured to care for me for as long as she had -- I thought if I said those words to her, I would never stop crying again. Because she had saved me. And I had not saved her.

I'm a journalist, and I've been writing and researching human trafficking for the past eight years or so, and even so, I never put together this personal story with my professional life until pretty recently. I think this profound disconnect actually symbolizes most of our understanding about human trafficking. Because human trafficking is far more prevalent, complex and close to home than most of us realize.

I spent time in jails and brothels, interviewed hundreds of survivors and law enforcement, NGO workers. And when I think about what we've done about human trafficking, I am hugely disappointed. Partly because we don't even talk about the problem right at all. When I say "human trafficking," most of you probably don't think about someone like my auntie. You probably think about a young girl or woman, who's been brutally forced into prostitution by a violent pimp. That is real suffering, and that is a real story. That story makes me angry for far more than just the reality of that situation, though.

As a journalist, I really care about how we relate to each other through language, and the way we tell that story, with all the gory, violent detail, the salacious aspects -- I call that "look at her scars" journalism. We use that story to convince ourselves that human trafficking is a bad man doing a bad thing to an innocent girl. That story lets us off the hook. It takes away all the societal context that we might be indicted for, for the structural inequality, or the poverty, or the barriers to migration. We let ourselves think that human trafficking is only about forced prostitution, when in reality, human trafficking is embedded in our everyday lives.

Let me show you what I mean. Forced prostitution accounts for 22 percent of human trafficking. Ten percent is in state- imposed forced labor. but a whopping 68 percent is for the purpose of creating the goods and delivering the services that most of us rely on every day, in sectors like agricultural work, domestic work and construction. That is food and care and shelter. And somehow, these most essential workers are also among the world's most underpaid and exploited today. Human trafficking is the use of force, fraud or coercion to compel another person's labor. And it's found in cotton fields, and coltan mines, and even car washes in Norway and England. It's found in U.S. military bases in Iraq and Afghanistan.

It's found in Thailand's fishing industry. That country has become the largest exporter of shrimp in the world. But what are the circumstances behind all that cheap and plentiful shrimp? Thai military were caught selling Burmese and Cambodian migrants onto fishing boats. Those fishing boats were taken out, the men put to work, and they were thrown overboard if they made the mistake of falling sick, or trying to resist their treatment. Those fish were then used to feed shrimp, the shrimp were then sold to four major global retailers: Costco, Tesco, Walmart and Carrefour.

Human trafficking is found on a smaller scale than just that, and in places you would never even imagine. Traffickers have forced young people to drive ice cream trucks, or to sing in touring boys' choirs. Trafficking has even been found in a hair braiding salon in New Jersey.

The scheme in that case was incredible. The traffickers found young families who were from Ghana and Togo, and they told these families that "your daughters are going to get a fine education in the United States." They then located winners of the green card lottery, and they told them, "We'll help you out. We'll get you a plane ticket. We'll pay your fees. All you have to do is take this young girl with you, say that she's your sister or your spouse. Once everyone arrived in New Jersey, the young girls were taken away, and put to work for 14-hour days, seven days a week, for five years. They made their traffickers nearly four million dollars.

This is a huge problem. So, what have we done about it? We've mostly turned to the criminal justice system. But keep in mind, most victims of human trafficking are poor and marginalized. They're migrants, people of color. Sometimes they're in the sex trade. And for populations like these, the criminal justice system is too often part of the problem, rather than the solution. In study after study, in countries ranging from Bangladesh to the United States, between 20 and 60 percent of the people in the sex trade who were surveyed said that they had been raped or assaulted by the police in the past year alone. People in prostitution, including people who have been trafficked into it, regularly receive multiple convictions for prostitution. Having that criminal record makes it so much more difficult to leave poverty, leave abuse, or leave prostitution, if that person so desires. Workers outside of the sex sector -- if they try and resist their treatment, they risk deportation. In case after case I've studied, employers have no problem calling on law enforcement to try and threaten or deport their striking trafficked workers. If those workers run away, they risk becoming part of the great mass of undocumented workers who are also subject to the whims of law enforcement if they're caught.

Law enforcement is supposed to identify victims and prosecute traffickers. But out of an estimated 21 million victims of human trafficking in the world, they have helped and identified fewer than 50,000 people. That's like comparing the population of the world to the population of Los Angeles, proportionally speaking. As for convictions, out of an estimated 5,700 convictions in 2013, fewer than 500 were for labor trafficking. Keep in mind that labor trafficking accounts for 68 percent of all trafficking, but fewer than 10 percent of the convictions.

I've heard one expert say that trafficking happens where need meets greed. I'd like to add one more element to that. Trafficking happens in sectors where workers are excluded from protections, and denied the right to organize. Trafficking doesn't happen in a vacuum. It happens in systematically degraded work environments. You might be thinking, oh, she's talking about failed states, or war-torn states, or -- I'm actually talking about the United States. Let me tell you what that looks like.

I spent many months researching a trafficking case called Global Horizons, involving hundreds of Thai farm workers. They were sent all over the States, to work in Hawaii pineapple plantations, and Washington apple orchards, and anywhere the work was needed. They were promised three years of solid agricultural work. So, they made a calculated risk. They sold their land, they sold their wives' jewelry, to make thousands in recruitment fees for this company, Global Horizons. But once they were brought over, their passports were confiscated. Some of the men were beaten and held at gunpoint. They worked so hard they fainted in the fields. This case hit me so hard.

After I came back home, I was wandering through the grocery store, and I froze in the produce department. I was remembering the over-the-top meals the Global Horizons survivors would make for me every time I showed up to interview them. They finished one meal with this plate of perfect, long-stemmed strawberries, and as they handed them to me, they said, "Aren't these the kind of strawberries you eat with somebody special in the States? And don't they taste so much better when you know the people whose hands picked them for you?"

As I stood in that grocery store weeks later, I realized I had no idea of who to thank for this plenty, and no idea of how they were being treated. So, like the journalist I am, I started digging into the agricultural sector. And I found there are too many fields, and too few labor inspectors. I found multiple layers of plausible deniability between grower and distributor and processor, and God knows who else. The Global Horizons survivors had been brought to the States on a temporary guest worker program. That guest worker program ties a person's legal status to his or her employer, and denies that worker the right to organize. Mind you, none of what I am describing about this agricultural sector or the guest worker program is actually human trafficking. It is merely what we find legally tolerable. And I would argue this is fertile ground for exploitation. And all of this had been hidden to me, before I had tried to understand it.

I wasn't the only person grappling with these issues. Pierre Omidyar, founder of eBay, is one of the biggest anti-trafficking philanthropists in the world. And even he wound up accidentally investing nearly 10 million dollars in the pineapple plantation cited as having the worst working conditions in that Global Horizons case. When he found out, he and his wife were shocked and horrified, and they wound up writing an op-ed for a newspaper, saying that it was up to all of us to learn everything we can about the labor and supply chains of the products that we support. I totally agree.

What would happen if each one of us decided that we are no longer going to support companies if they don't eliminate exploitation from their labor and supply chains? If we demanded laws calling for the same? If all the CEOs out there decided that they were going to go through their businesses and say, "no more"? If we ended recruitment fees for migrant workers? If we decided that guest workers should have the right to organize without fear of retaliation? These would be decisions heard around the world. This isn't a matter of buying a fair-trade peach and calling it a day, buying a guilt-free zone with your money. That's not how it works. This is the decision to change a system that is broken, and that we have unwittingly but willingly allowed ourselves to profit from and benefit from for too long.

We often dwell on human trafficking survivors' victimization. But that is not my experience of them. Over all the years that I've been talking to them, they have taught me that we are more than our worst days. Each one of us is more than what we have lived through. Especially trafficking survivors. These people were the most resourceful and resilient and responsible in their communities. They were the people that you would take a gamble on. You'd say, I'm going to sell my rings, because I have the chance to send you off to a better future. They were the emissaries of hope.

These survivors don't need saving. They need solidarity, because they're behind some of the most exciting social justice movements out there today. The nannies and housekeepers who marched with their families and their employers' families -- their activism got us an international treaty on domestic workers' rights. The Nepali women who were trafficked into the sex trade -- they came together, and they decided that they were going to make the world's first anti-trafficking organization actually headed and run by trafficking survivors themselves. These Indian shipyard workers were trafficked to do post-Hurricane Katrina reconstruction. They were threatened with deportation, but they broke out of their work compound and they marched from New Orleans to Washington,

D.C., to protest labor exploitation. They cofounded an organization called the National Guest Worker Alliance, and through this organization, they have wound up helping other workers bring to light exploitation and abuses in supply chains in Walmart and Hershey's factories. And although the Department of Justice declined to take their case, a team of civil rights lawyers won the first of a dozen civil suits this February, and got their clients 14 million dollars.

These survivors are fighting for people they don't even know yet, other workers, and for the possibility of a just world for all of us. This is our chance to do the same. This is our chance to make the decision that tells us who we are, as a people and as a society; that our prosperity is no longer prosperity, as long as it is pinned to other people's pain; that our lives are inextricably woven together; and that we have the power to make a different choice.

I was so reluctant to share my story of my auntie with you. I had told literally a handful of people about it, because, like many a journalist, I am far more interested in learning about your stories than sharing much, if anything, about my own. I also haven't done my journalistic due diligence on this. I haven't issued my mountains of document requests, and interviewed everyone and their mother, and I haven't found my auntie yet. I don't know her story of what happened, and of her life now. The story as I've told it to you is messy and unfinished. But I think it mirrors the messy and unfinished situation we're all in, when it comes to human trafficking. We are all implicated in this problem. But that means we are all also part of its solution. Figuring out how to build a more just world is our work to do, and our story to tell. So, let us tell it the way we should have done, from the very beginning. Let us tell this story together.

Chapter 8
Why we need to end the era of orphanages [8]

It all started for me when I was 19 years old and went backpacking through Southeast Asia. When I reached Cambodia, I felt uncomfortable being on holiday surrounded by so much poverty and wanted to do something to give back. So, I visited some orphanages and donated some clothes and books and some money to help the kids that I met.

But one of the orphanages I visited was desperately poor. I had never encountered poverty like that before in my life. They didn't have funds for enough food, clean water or medical treatment, and the sad little faces on those kids were heartbreaking. So, I was compelled to do something more to help. I fund-raised in Australia and returned to Cambodia the following year to volunteer at the orphanage for a few months. I taught English

---

[8] Tara winkler: How (Not) to Start an Orphanage: By a Woman Who Did, amazon 2016.

and bought water filters and food and took all of the kids to the dentist for the first time in their lives.

But over the course of the next year, I came to discover that this orphanage that I had been supporting was terribly corrupt. The director had been embezzling every cent donated to the orphanage, and in my absence, the children were suffering such gross neglect that they were forced to catch mice to feed themselves. I also found out later that the director had been physically and sexually abusing the kids. I couldn't bring myself to turn my back on children who I had come to know and care about and return to my life in Australia. So I worked with a local team and the local authorities to set up a new orphanage and rescue the kids to give them a safe new home.

But this is where my story takes another unexpected turn. As I adjusted to my new life running an orphanage in Cambodia, (Khmer) I learned to speak Khmer fluently, which means that I learned to speak the Khmer language fluently. And when I could communicate properly with the kids, I began to uncover some strange things. Most of the children we had removed from the orphanage were not, in fact, orphans at all. They had parents, and the few that were orphaned had other living relatives, like grandparents and aunties and uncles and other siblings.

So why were these children living in an orphanage when they weren't orphans? Since 2005, the number of orphanages in Cambodia has risen by 75 percent, and the number of children living in Cambodian orphanages has nearly doubled, despite the fact that the vast majority of children living in these orphanages are not orphans in the traditional sense. They're children from poor families. So, if the vast majority of children living in orphanages are not orphans, then the term "orphanage" is really just a euphemistic name for a residential care institution. These institutions go by other names as well, like "shelters," "safe houses," "children's homes," "children's villages," even "boarding schools."

And this problem is not just confined to Cambodia. This map shows some of the countries that have seen a dramatic increase in the numbers of residential care institutions and the numbers of children being institutionalized. In Uganda, for example, the number of children living in institutions has increased by more than 1,600 percent since 1992. And the problems posed by putting kids into institutions don't just pertain to the corrupt and abusive institutions like the one that I rescued the kids from. The problems are with all forms of residential care.

Over 60 years of international research has shown us that children who grow up in institutions, even the very best institutions, are at serious risk of developing mental illnesses, attachment disorders, growth and speech delays, and many will struggle with an inability to reintegrate back into society later in life and form healthy relationships as adults. These kids grow up without any model of family or of what good parenting looks like, so they then can struggle to parent their own children. So, if you institutionalize large numbers of children, it will affect not only this generation, but also the generations to come.

We've learned these lessons before in Australia. It's what happened to our "Stolen Generations," the indigenous children who were removed from their families with the belief that we could do a better job of raising their children.

Just imagine for a moment what residential care would be like for a child. Firstly, you have a constant rotation of caregivers, with somebody new coming on to the shift every eight hours. And then on top of that you have a steady stream of visitors and volunteers coming in, showering you in the love and affection you're craving and then leaving again, evoking all of those feelings of abandonment, and proving again and again that you are not worthy of being loved.

We don't have orphanages in Australia, the USA, the UK anymore, and for a very good reason: one study has shown that young adults raised in institutions are 10 times more likely to fall into sex work than their peers, 40 times more likely to have a criminal record, and 500 times more likely to take their own lives. There are an estimated eight million children around the world living in institutions like orphanages, despite the fact that around 80 percent of them are not orphans. Most have families who could be caring for them if they had the right support.

But for me, the most shocking thing of all to realize is what's contributing to this boom in the unnecessary institutionalization of so many children: it's us -- the tourists, the volunteers and the donors. It's the well-meaning support from people like me back in 2006, who visit these children and volunteer and donate, who are unwittingly fueling an industry that exploits children and tears families apart.

It's really no coincidence that these institutions are largely set up in areas where tourists can most easily be lured in to visit and volunteer in exchange for donations. Of the 600 so-called orphanages in Nepal, over 90 percent of them are located in the most popular tourist hotspots. The cold, hard truth is, the more money that floods in in support of these institutions, the more institutions open and the more children are removed from their families to fill their beds. It's just the laws of supply and demand.

I had to learn all of these lessons the hard way, after I had already set up an orphanage in Cambodia. I had to eat a big piece of humble pie to admit that I had made a mistake and inadvertently become a part of the problem. I had been an orphanage tourist, a voluntourist. I then set up my own orphanage and facilitated orphanage tourism in order to generate funds for my orphanage, before I knew better. What I came to learn is that no matter how good my orphanage was, it was never going to give those kids what they really needed: their families.

I know that it can feel incredibly depressing to learn that helping vulnerable children and overcoming poverty is not as simple as we've all been led to believe it should be. But thankfully, there is a solution. These problems are reversible and preventable, and when we know better, we can do better.

The organization that I run today, the Cambodian Children's Trust, is no longer an orphanage. In 2012, we changed the model in favor of family-based care. I now lead an amazing team of Cambodian social workers, nurses and teachers. Together, we work within communities to untangle a complex web of social issues and help Cambodian families escape poverty. Our primary focus is on preventing some of the most vulnerable families in our community from being separated in the first place. But in cases where it's not possible for a child to live with its biological family, we support them in foster care. Family-based care is always better than placing a child in an institution.

Do you remember that first photo that I showed you before? See that girl who is just about to catch the ball? Her name is Torn She's a strong, brave and fiercely intelligent girl. But in 2006, when I first met her living in that corrupt and abusive orphanage, she had never been to school. She was suffering terrible neglect, and she yearned desperately for the warmth and love of her mother. But this is a photo of Torn today with her family. Her mother now has a secure job, her siblings are doing well in high school and she is just about to finish her nursing degree at university. For Torn's family the cycle of poverty has been broken. The family-based care model that we have developed at CCT has been so successful, that it's now being put forward by UNICEF Cambodia and the Cambodian government as a national solution to keep children in families. And one of the best ways that you can help to solve this problem is by giving these eight million children a voice and become an advocate for family-based care.

If we work together to raise awareness, we can make sure the world knows that we need to put an end to the unnecessary institutionalization of vulnerable children. How do we achieve that? By redirecting our support and our donations away from orphanages and residential care institutions towards organizations that are committed to keeping children in families.

I believe we can make this happen in our lifetime, and as a result, we will see developing communities thrive and ensure that vulnerable children everywhere have what all children need and deserve: a family.

Chapter 9
An ode to envy [9]

when I was eight years old, a new girl came to join the class, and she was so impressive, as the new girl always seems to be. She had vast quantities of very shiny hair and a cute little pencil case, super strong on state capitals, just a great speller. And I just curdled with jealousy that year, until I hatched my devious plan. So, one day I stayed a little late after school, a little too late, and I lurked in the girls' bathroom. When the coast was clear, I emerged, crept into the classroom, and took from my teacher's desk the grade book. And then I did it. I fiddled with my rival's grades, just a little, just demoted some of those A's. All of those A's. And I got ready to return the book to the drawer, when hang on, some of my other classmates had appallingly good grades too. So, in a frenzy, I corrected everybody's marks, not imaginatively. I gave

---

)9 Parul sehgal: literary critic, editor for the new York times book review.

everybody a row of D's and I gave myself a row of A's, just because I was there, you know, might as well.

And I am still baffled by my behavior. I don't understand where the idea came from. I don't understand why I felt so great doing it. I felt great. I don't understand why I was never caught. I mean, it should have been so blatantly obvious. I was never caught. But most of all, I am baffled by, why did it bother me so much that this little girl, this tiny little girl, was so good at spelling? Jealousy baffles me. It's so mysterious, and it's so pervasive. We know babies suffer from jealousy. We know primates do. Bluebirds are actually very prone. We know that jealousy is the number one cause of spousal murder in the United States. And yet, I have never read a study that can parse to me its loneliness or its longevity or its grim thrill. For that, we have to go to fiction, because the novel is the lab that has studied jealousy in every possible configuration. In fact, I don't know if it's an exaggeration to say that if we didn't have jealousy, would we even have literature? Well no faithless Helen, no "Odyssey." No jealous king, no "Arabian Nights." No Shakespeare. There go high school reading lists, because we're losing "Sound and the Fury," we're losing "Gatsby," "Sun Also Rises," we're losing "Madame Bovary," "Anna K." No jealousy, no Proust. And now, I mean, I know it's fashionable to say that Proust has the answers to everything, but in the case of jealousy, he kind of does. This year is the centennial of his masterpiece, "In Search of Lost Time," and it's the most exhaustive study of sexual jealousy and just regular competitiveness, my brand, that we can hope to have. And we think about Proust, we think about the sentimental bits, right? We think about a little boy trying to get to sleep. We think about a madeleine moistened in lavender tea. We forget how harsh his vision was. We forget how pitiless he is. I mean, these are books that Virginia Woolf said were tough as cat gut. I don't know what cat gut is, but let's assume it's formidable.

Let's look at why they go so well together, the novel and jealousy, jealousy and Proust. Is it something as obvious as that jealousy, which boils down into person, desire, impediment, is such a solid narrative foundation? I don't know. I think it cuts very close to the bone, because let's think about what happens when we feel jealous. When we feel jealous, we tell ourselves a story. We tell ourselves a story about other people's lives, and these stories make us feel terrible because they're designed to make us feel terrible. As the teller of the tale and the audience, we know just what details to include, to dig that knife in. Right? Jealousy makes us all amateur novelists, and this is something Proust understood.

In the first volume, Swann's Way, the series of books, Swann, one of the main characters, is thinking very fondly of his mistress and how great she is in bed, and suddenly, in the course of a few sentences, and these are Proustian sentences, so they're long as rivers, but in the course of a few sentences, he suddenly recoils and he realizes, "Hang on, everything I love about this woman, somebody else would love about this woman. Everything that she does that gives me pleasure could be giving somebody else pleasure, maybe right about now." And this is the story he starts to tell himself, and from then on, Proust writes that every fresh charm Swann detects in his mistress, he adds to his "collection of instruments in his private torture chamber."

Now Swann and Proust, we have to admit, were notoriously jealous. You know, Proust's boyfriends would have to leave the country if they wanted to break up with him. But you don't have to be that jealous to concede that it's hard work. Right? Jealousy is exhausting. It's a hungry emotion. It must be fed.

And what does jealousy like? Jealousy likes information. Jealousy likes details. Jealousy likes the vast quantities of shiny hair, the cute little pencil case. Jealousy likes photos. That's why Instagram is such a hit. (Laughter) Proust actually links the language of scholarship and jealousy. When Swann is in his jealous throes, and suddenly he's listening at doorways and bribing his mistress' servants, he defends these behaviors. He says, "You know, look, I know you think this is repugnant, but it is no different from interpreting an ancient text or looking at a monument." He says, "They are scientific investigations with real intellectual value." Proust is trying to show us that jealousy feels intolerable and makes us look absurd, but it is, at its crux, a quest for knowledge, a quest for truth, painful truth, and actually, where Proust is concerned, the more painful the truth, the better. Grief, humiliation, loss: These were the avenues to wisdom for Proust. He says, "A woman whom we need, who makes us suffer, elicits from us a gamut of feelings far more profound and vital than a man of genius who interests us." Is he telling us to just go and find cruel women? No. I think he's trying to say that jealousy reveals us to ourselves. And does any other emotion crack us open in this particular way? Does any other emotion reveal to us our aggression and our hideous ambition and our entitlement? Does any other emotion teach us to look with such peculiar intensity?

Freud would write about this later. One day, Freud was visited by this very anxious young man who was consumed with the thought of his wife cheating on him. And Freud says, it's something strange about this guy, because he's not looking at what his wife is doing. Because she's blameless; everybody knows it. The poor creature is just under suspicion for no cause. But he's looking for things that his wife is doing without noticing, unintentional behaviors. Is she smiling too brightly here, or did she accidentally brush up against a man there? [Freud] says that the man is becoming the custodian of his wife's unconscious.

The novel is very good on this point. The novel is very good at describing how jealousy trains us to look with intensity but not accuracy. In fact, the more intensely jealous we are, the more we become residents of fantasy. And this is why, I think, jealousy doesn't just provoke us to do violent things or illegal things. Jealousy prompts us to behave in ways that are wildly inventive. Now I'm thinking of myself at eight, I concede, but I'm also thinking of this story I heard on the news. A 52-year-old Michigan woman was caught creating a fake Facebook account from which she sent vile, hideous messages to herself for a year. For a year. A year. And she was trying to frame her ex-boyfriend's new girlfriend, and I have to confess when I heard this, I just reacted with admiration. Because, I mean, let's be real. What immense, if misplaced, creativity. Right? This is something from a novel. This is something from a Patricia Highsmith novel.

Now Highsmith is a particular favorite of mine. She is the very brilliant and bizarre woman of American letters. She's the author of "Strangers on a Train" and "The Talented Mr. Ripley," books that are all about how jealousy, it muddles our minds, and once we're in the sphere, in that realm of jealousy, the membrane between what is and what could be can be pierced in an instant. Take Tom Ripley, her most famous character. Now, Tom Ripley goes from wanting you or wanting what you have to being you and having what you once had, and you're under the floorboards, he's answering to your name, he's wearing your rings, emptying your bank account. That's one way to go.

But what do we do? We can't go the Tom Ripley route. I can't give the world D's, as much as I would really like to, some days. And it's a pity, because we live in envious times. We live in jealous times. I mean, we're all good citizens of social media, aren't we, where the currency is envy?

Does the novel show us a way out? I'm not sure. So, let's do what characters always do when they're not sure, when they are in possession of a mystery. Let's go to 221B Baker Street and ask for Sherlock Holmes. When people think of Holmes, they think of his nemesis being Professor Moriarty, right, this criminal mastermind. But I've always preferred [Inspector] Lestrade, who is the rat-faced head of Scotland Yard who needs Holmes desperately, needs Holmes' genius, but resents him. Oh, it's so familiar to me. So Lestrade needs his help, resents him, and sort of seethes with bitterness over the course of the mysteries. But as they work together, something starts to change, and finally in "The Adventure of the Six Napoleons," once Holmes comes in, dazzles everybody with his solution, Lestrade turns to Holmes and he says, "We're not jealous of you, Mr. Holmes. We're proud of you." And he says that there's not a man at Scotland Yard who wouldn't want to shake Sherlock Holmes' hand.

It's one of the few times we see Holmes moved in the mysteries, and I find it very moving, this little scene, but it's also mysterious, right? It seems to treat jealousy as a problem of geometry, not emotion. You know, one-minute Holmes is on the other side from Lestrade. The next minute they're on the same side. Suddenly, Lestrade is letting himself admire this mind that he's resented. Could it be so simple though? What if jealousy really is a matter of geometry, just a matter of where we allow ourselves to stand in relation to another? Well, maybe then we wouldn't have to resent somebody's excellence. We could align ourselves with it.

But I like contingency plans. So, while we wait for that to happen, let us remember that we have fiction for consolation. Fiction alone demystifies jealousy. Fiction alone domesticates it, invites it to the table. And look who it gathers: sweet Lestrade, terrifying Tom Ripley, crazy Swann, Marcel Proust himself. We are in excellent company.

Chapter 10
In praise of slowness [10]

What I'd like to start off with is an observation, which is that if I've learned anything over the last year, it's that the supreme irony of publishing a book about slowness is that you have to go around promoting it really fast. I seem to spend most of my time these days zipping from city to city, studio to studio, interview to interview, serving up the book in really tiny bite-size chunks. Because everyone these days wants to know how to slow down, but they want to know how to slow down really quickly. So ... so I did a spot-on CNN the other day where I actually spent more time in makeup than I did talking on air. And I think that -- that's not really surprising though, is it? Because that's kind of the world that we live in now, a world stuck in fast-forward.

A world obsessed with speed, with doing everything faster, with cramming more

---

)[10] carl honore: writer, thinker, activist.

and more into less and less time. Every moment of the day feels like a race against the clock. To borrow a phrase from Carrie Fisher, which is in my bio there; I'll just toss it out again -- "These days even instant gratification takes too long. And if you think about how we to try to make things better, what do we do? No, we speed them up, don't we? So, we used to dial; now we speed dial. We used to read; now we speed read. We used to walk; now we speed walk. And of course, we used to date and now we speed date. And even things that are by their very nature slow -- we try and speed them up too. So, I was in New York recently, and I walked past a gym that had an advertisement in the window for a new course, a new evening course. And it was for, you guessed it, speed yoga. So, this -- the perfect solution for time-starved professionals who want to, you know, salute the sun, but only want to give over about 20 minutes to it. I mean, these are sort of the extreme examples, and they're amusing and good to laugh at.

But there's a very serious point, and I think that in the headlong dash of daily life, we often lose sight of the damage that this roadrunner form of living does to us. We're so marinated in the culture of speed that we almost fail to notice the toll it takes on every aspect of our lives -- on our health, our diet, our work, our relationships, the environment and our community. And sometimes it takes a wake-up call, doesn't it, to alert us to the fact that we're hurrying through our lives, instead of actually living them; that we're living the fast life, instead of the good life. And I think for many people, that wake-up call takes the form of an illness. You know, a burnout, or eventually the body says, "I can't take it anymore," and throws in the towel. Or maybe a relationship goes up in smoke because we haven't had the time, or the patience, or the tranquility, to be with the other person, to listen to them.

And my wake-up call came when I started reading bedtime stories to my son, and I found that at the end of day, I would go into his room and I just couldn't slow down -- you know, I'd be speed reading "The Cat In The Hat." I'd be -- you know, I'd be skipping lines here, paragraphs there, sometimes a whole page, and of course, my little boy knew the book inside out, so we would quarrel. And what should have been the most relaxing, the most intimate, the most tender moment of the day, when a dad sits down to read to his son, became instead this kind of gladiatorial battle of wills, a clash between my speed and his slowness. And this went on for some time, until I caught myself scanning a newspaper article with timesaving tips for fast people. And one of them made reference to a series of books called "The One-Minute Bedtime Story." And I wince saying those words now, but my first reaction at the time was very different. My first reflex was to say, "Hallelujah -- what a great idea! This is exactly what I'm looking for to speed up bedtime even more." But thankfully, a light bulb went on over my head, and my next reaction was very different, and I took a step back, and I thought, "Whoa -- you know, has it really come to this? Am I really in such a hurry that I'm prepared to fob off my son with a sound byte at the end of the day?" And I put away the newspaper -- and I was getting on a plane -- and I sat there, and I did something I hadn't done for a long time -- which is I did nothing. I just thought, and I thought long and hard. And by the time I got off that plane, I'd decided I wanted to do something about it. I wanted to investigate this whole roadrunner culture, and what it was doing to me and to everyone else.

And I had two questions in my head. The first was, how did we get so fast? And the second is, is it possible, or even desirable, to slow down? Now, if you think about how our world got so accelerated, the usual suspects rear their heads. You think of, you know, urbanization, consumerism, the workplace, technology. But I think if you cut through those forces, you get to what might be the deeper driver, the nub of the question, which is how we think about time itself. In other cultures, time is cyclical. It's seen as moving in great, unhurried circles. It's always renewing and refreshing itself. Whereas in the West, time is linear. It's a finite resource; it's always draining away. You either use it, or lose it. "Time is money," as Benjamin Franklin said. And I think what that does to us psychologically is it creates an equation. Time is scarce, so what do we do? Well -- well, we speed up, don't we? We try and do more and more with less and less time. We turn every moment of every day into a race to the finish line -- a finish line, incidentally, that we never reach, but a finish line nonetheless. And I guess that the question is, is it possible to break free from that mindset? And thankfully, the answer is yes, because what I discovered, when I began looking around, that there is a global backlash against this culture that tells us that faster is always better, and that busier is best.

Right across the world, people are doing the unthinkable: they're slowing down, and finding that, although conventional wisdom tells you that if you slow down, you're road kill, the opposite turns out to be true: that by slowing down at the right moments, people find that they do everything better. They eat better; they make love better; they exercise better; they work better; they live better. And, in this kind of cauldron of moments and places and acts of deceleration, lie what a lot of people now refer to as the "International Slow Movement."

Now if you'll permit me a small act of hypocrisy, I'll just give you a very quick overview of what's going on inside the Slow Movement. If you think of food, many of you will have heard of the Slow Food movement. Started in Italy, but has spread across the world, and now has 100,000 members in 50 countries. And it's driven by a very simple and sensible message, which is that we get more pleasure and more health from our food when we cultivate, cook and consume it at a reasonable pace. I think also the explosion of the organic farming movement, and the renaissance of farmers' markets, are other illustrations of the fact that people are desperate to get away from eating and cooking and cultivating their food on an industrial timetable. They want to get back to slower rhythms. And out of the Slow Food movement has grown something called the Slow Cities movement, which has started in Italy, but has spread right across Europe and beyond. And in this, towns begin to rethink how they organize the urban landscape, so that people are encouraged to slow down and smell the roses and connect with one another. So, they might curb traffic, or put in a park bench, or some green space.

And in some ways, these changes add up to more than the sum of their parts, because I think when a Slow City becomes officially a Slow City, it's kind of like a philosophical declaration. It's saying to the rest of world, and to the people in that town, that we believe that in the 21st century, slowness has a role to play. In medicine, I think a lot of people are deeply disillusioned with the kind of quick-fix mentality you find in conventional medicine. And millions of them around the world are turning to complementary and alternative forms of medicine, which tend to tap into sort of slower, gentler, more holistic forms of healing. Now, obviously the jury is out on many of these complementary therapies, and I personally doubt that the coffee enema will ever, you know, gain mainstream approval. But other treatments such as acupuncture and massage, and even just relaxation, clearly have some kind of benefit. And blue-chip medical colleges everywhere are starting to study these things to find out how they work, and what we might learn from them.

Sex. There's an awful lot of fast sex around, isn't there? I was coming to -- well -- no pun intended there. I was making my way, let's say, slowly to Oxford, and I went through a news agent, and I saw a magazine, a men's magazine, and it said on the front, "How to bring your partner to orgasm in 30 seconds." So, you know, even sex is on a stopwatch these days. Now, you know, I like a quickie as much as the next person, but I think that there's an awful lot to be gained from slow sex -- from slowing down in the bedroom. You know, you tap into that -- those deeper, sort of, psychological, emotional, spiritual currents, and you get a better orgasm with the buildup. You can get more bang for your buck, let's say. I mean, the Pointer Sisters said it most eloquently, didn't they, when they sang the praises of "a lover with a slow hand." Now, we all laughed at Sting a few years ago when he went Tantric, but you fast-forward a few years, and now you find couples of all ages flocking to workshops, or maybe just on their own in their own bedrooms, finding ways to put on the brakes and have better sex. And of course, in Italy where -- I mean, Italians always seem to know where to find their pleasure -- they've launched an official Slow Sex movement.

The workplace. Right across much of the world -- North America being a notable exception -- working hours have been coming down. And Europe is an example of that, and people finding that their quality of life improves as they're working less, and also that their hourly productivity goes up. Now, clearly there are problems with the 35-hour workweek in France -- too much, too soon, too rigid. But other countries in Europe, notably the Nordic countries, are showing that it's possible to have a kick-ass economy without being a workaholic. And Norway, Sweden, Denmark and Finland now rank among the top six most competitive nations on Earth, and they work the kind of hours that would make the average American weep with envy. And if you go beyond sort of the country level, down at the micro-company level, more and more companies now are realizing that they need to allow their staff either to work fewer hours or just to unplug -- to take a lunch break, or to go sit in a quiet room, to switch off their Blackberries and laptops -- you at the back -- mobile phones, during the work day or on the weekend, so that they have time to recharge and for the brain to slide into that kind of creative mode of thought.

It's not just, though, these days, adults who overwork, though, is it? It's children, too. I'm 37, and my childhood ended in the mid-'80s, and I look at kids now, and I'm just amazed by the way they race around with more homework, more tutoring, more extracurriculars than we would ever have conceived of a generation ago. And some of the most heartrending emails that I get on my website are actually from adolescents hovering on the edge of burnout, pleading with me to write to their parents, to help them slow down, to help them get off this full-throttle treadmill. But thankfully, there is a backlash there in parenting as well, and you're finding that, you know, towns in the United States are now banding together and banning extracurriculars on a particular day of the month, so that people can, you know, decompress and have some family time, and slow down.

Homework is another thing. There are homework bans springing up all over the developed world in schools which had been piling on the homework for years, and now they're discovering that less can be more. So there was a case up in Scotland recently where a fee-paying, high-achieving private school banned homework for everyone under the age of 13, and the high-achieving parents freaked out and said, "What are you -- you know, our kids will fall" -- the headmaster said, "No, no, your children need to slow down at the end of the day." And just this last month, the exam results came in, and in math, science, marks went up 20 percent on average last year. And I think what's very revealing is that the elite universities, who are often cited as the reason that people drive their kids and hothouse them so much, are starting to notice the caliber of students coming to them is falling. These kids have wonderful marks; they have CVs jammed with extracurriculars, to the point that would make your eyes water. But they lack spark; they lack the ability to think creatively and think outside -- they don't know how to dream. And so, what these Ivy League schools, and Oxford and Cambridge and so on, are starting to send a message to parents and students that they need to put on the brakes a little bit. And in Harvard, for instance, they send out a letter to undergraduates -- freshmen -- telling them that they'll get more out of life, and more out of Harvard, if they put on the brakes, if they do less, but give time to things, the time that things need, to enjoy them, to savor them. And even if they sometimes do nothing at all. And that letter is called -- very revealing, I think -- "Slow Down!" -- with an exclamation mark on the end.

So, wherever you look, the message, it seems to me, is the same: that less is very often more, that slower is very often better. But that said, of course, it's not that easy to slow down, is it? I mean, you heard that I got a speeding ticket while I was researching my book on the benefits of slowness, and that's true, but that's not all of it. I was actually in route to a dinner held by Slow Food at the time. And if that's not shaming enough, I got that ticket in Italy. And if any of you have ever driven on an

Italian highway, you'll have a pretty good idea of how fast I was going.

But why is it so hard to slow down? I think there are various reasons. One is that speed is fun, you know, speed is sexy. It's all that adrenaline rush. It's hard to give it up. I think there's a kind of metaphysical dimension -- that speed becomes a way of walling ourselves off from the bigger, deeper questions. We fill our head with distraction, with busyness, so that we don't have to ask, am I well? Am I happy? Are my children growing up right? Are politicians making good decisions on my behalf? Another reason -- although I think, perhaps, the most powerful reason -- why we find it hard to slow down is the cultural taboo that we've erected against slowing down. "Slow" is a dirty word in our culture. It's a byword for "lazy," "slacker," for being somebody who gives up. You know, "he's a bit slow." It's actually synonymous with being stupid.

I guess what the Slow Movement -- the purpose of the Slow Movement, or its main goal, really, is to tackle that taboo, and to say that yes, sometimes slow is not the answer, that there is such a thing as "bad slow." You know, I got stuck on the M25, which is a ring road around London, recently, and spent three-and-a-half hours there. And I can tell you, that's really bad slow. But the new idea, the sort of revolutionary idea, of the Slow Movement, is that there is such a thing as "good slow," too. And good slow is, you know, taking the time to eat a meal with your family, with the TV switched off. Or taking the time to look at a problem from all angles in the office to make the best decision at work. Or even simply just taking the time to slow down and savor your life.

Now, one of the things that I found most uplifting about all of this stuff that's happened around the book since it came out, is the reaction to it. And I knew that when my book on slowness came out, it would be welcomed by the New Age brigade, but it's also been taken up, with great gusto, by the corporate world -- you know, business press, but also big companies and leadership organizations. Because people at the top of the chain, people like you, I think, are starting to realize that there's too much speed in the system, there's too much busyness, and it's time to find, or get back to that lost art of shifting gears. Another encouraging sign, I think, is that it's not just in the developed world that this idea's been taken up. In the developing world, in countries that are on the verge of making that leap into first world status -- China, Brazil, Thailand, Poland, and so on -- these countries have embraced the idea of the Slow Movement, many people in them, and there's a debate going on in their media, on the streets. Because I think they're looking at the West, and they're saying, "Well, we like that aspect of what you've got, but we're not so sure about that."

So, all of that said, is it, I guess, is it possible? That's really the main question before us today. Is it possible to slow down? And I'm happy to be able to say to you that the answer is a resounding yes. And I present myself as Exhibit A, a kind of reformed and rehabilitated speed-aholic. I still love speed. You know, I live in London, and I work as a journalist, and I enjoy the buzz and the busyness, and the adrenaline rush that comes from both of those things. I play squash and ice hockey, two very fast sports, and I wouldn't give them up for the world. But I've also, over the last year or so, got in touch with my inner tortoise.

And what that means is that I no longer overload myself gratuitously. My default mode is no longer to be a rush-aholic. I no longer hear time's winged chariot drawing near, or at least not as much as I did before. I can actually hear it now, because I see my time is ticking off. And the upshot of all of that is that I actually feel a lot happier, healthier, more productive than I ever have. I feel like I'm living my life rather than actually just racing through it. And perhaps, the most important measure of the success of this is that I feel that my relationships are a lot deeper, richer, stronger.

And for me, I guess, the litmus test for whether this would work, and what it would mean, was always going to be bedtime stories, because that's sort of where the journey began. And there too the news is rosy. You know, at the end of the day, I go into my son's room. I don't wear a watch. I switch off my computer, so I can't hear the email pinging into the basket, and I just slow down to his pace and we read. And because children have their own tempo and internal clock, they don't do quality time, where you schedule 10 minutes for them to open up to you. They need you to move at their rhythm. I find that 10 minutes into a story, you know, my son will suddenly say, "You know, something happened in the playground today that really bothered me." And we'll go off and have a conversation on that. And I now find that bedtime stories used to be a box on my to-do list, something that I dreaded, because it was so slow and I had to get through it quickly. It's become my reward at the end of the day, something I really cherish. And I have a kind of Hollywood ending to my talk this afternoon, which goes a little bit like this:

a few months ago, I was getting ready to go on another book tour, and I had my bags packed. I was downstairs by the front door, and I was waiting for a taxi, and my son came down the stairs and he'd made a card for me. And he was carrying it. He'd gone and stapled two cards, very like these, together, and put a sticker of his favorite character, Tintin, on the front. And he said to me, or he handed this to me, and I read it, and it said, "To Daddy, love

Benjamin." And I thought, "Aw, that's really sweet. Is that a good luck on the book tour card?" And he said, "No, no, no, Daddy -- this is a card for being the best story reader in the world." And I thought, "Yeah, you know, this slowing down thing really does work."

References

1. steven pinker: Enlightenment Now: The Case for Reason, Science, Humanism, and Progress. Amazon, 2018

2. William macaskill: Doing Good Better: How Effective Altruism Can Help You Help Others, Do Work that Matters, and Make Smarter Choices about Giving Back. Amazon, 2016

3. ozlem cekic: bridge builder, author.

4. Zachary R.wood: Uncensored: My Life and Uncomfortable Conversations at the Intersection of Black and White America. Amazon 2018

5. barry schwartz: Why We Work (TED Books). Amazon, 2015

6. musimbi kanyoro: women's rights activist.

7. noy thrupkaew: global journalist.

8. tara winkler: How (Not) to Start an Orphanage: By a Woman Who Did, amazon 2016.

9. parul sehgal: literary critic, editor for the New York times book review.

10.   carl honore: writer, thinker, activist.